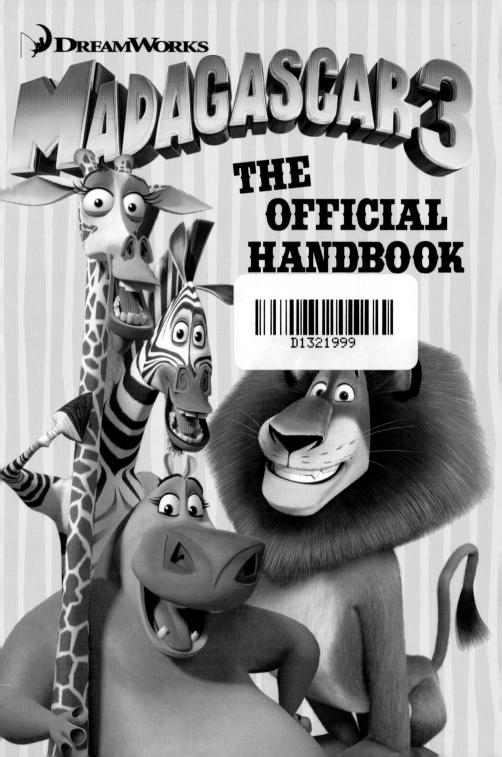

DREAMWORKS

MADAGASCAR 3

THE OFFICIAL HANDBOOK

D1321999

MADAGASCAR 3: THE OFFICIAL HANDBOOK
A BANTAM BOOK 978 0 857 51135 5

First published in Great Britain by Bantam,
an imprint of Random House Children's Publishers UK
A Random House Group Company

This edition published 2012

1 3 5 7 9 10 8 6 4 2

Madagascar 3 © DreamWorks Animation L.L.C.

The Random House Group Limited supports the Forest Stewardship Council (FSC®), the leading international forest
certification organization. Our books carrying the FSC label are printed on FSC®-certified paper. FSC is the only forest
certification scheme endorsed by the leading environmental organizations, including Greenpeace. Our paper procurement
policy can be found at www.randomhouse.co.uk/environment.

Bantam Books are published by Random House Children's Publishers UK,
61–63 Uxbridge Road, London W5 5SA

www.randomhousechildrens.co.uk
www.randomhouse.co.uk

Addresses for companies within The Random House Group Limited can be found at: www.randomhouse.co.uk/offices.htm

THE RANDOM HOUSE GROUP Limited Reg. No. 954009

A CIP catalogue record for this book is available from the British Library.

Printed in China

CONTENTS

A TASTE OF FREEDOM . . .

'Just imagine going back to nature, back to your roots, clean air, wide open spaces!'

Life was easy at the New York Zoo. Alex the lion was the star of the show, Melman the giraffe had his own team of personal doctors, and Gloria the hippo loved hanging out in her watering hole. But on his tenth birthday, when Marty the zebra learnt that the Penguins were planning to break out of the zoo, he yearned for freedom in the wild.

'So what are you gonna do, just go running off to the wild by yourself?'

Later that night, the animals discovered that Marty's pen was empty — he'd made a run for it! Gloria smashed a hole through the zoo wall and the friends hurried to Grand Central Station to stop him from leaving the city.

They found Marty at the train station, but were suddenly cornered by the police. Unfortunately four wild animals really stand out on the streets of New York City! Alex tried to explain why they were there, but the police had tranquillizer guns and the Zoosters were soon knocked out cold.

DID YOU KNOW?
Madagascar is the world's fourth largest island.

ZOO WHO?
Which of these is not an animal kept at New York Zoo?

1. Mouse deer
2. Bufflehead duck
3. Ruzzy Cat
4. Pig-nosed turtle
5. Fruit Bat

Answer: 3

5

A NEW HOME

'White sandy beaches, a cleverly simulated natural environment, complete with fake rocks. We must be in San Diego.'

The zoo decided to transfer Alex and his friends to a wildlife preserve in Kenya, but things went wrong on the journey when the Penguins took over the ship and set sail for Antarctica. The crates containing Alex, Marty, Melman and Gloria fell off the boat!

The next thing the Zoosters knew, their crates washed up on a beautiful beach. Marty was overjoyed but the others weren't so pleased. Especially when they ran into a crazy pack of lemurs. Their leader, King Julien, first thought the Zoosters were a threat but soon realised they were friendly.

After a while, the four friends started to like being in the wild. The more Alex enjoyed himself however, the more his hunting instincts began to show. He was used to being pampered in the zoo and eating lots of steak, but things were very different in the wild.

King Julien decided the Zoosters could help them scare off their enemies, the fossa. Unfortunately, Alex's hunger got the better of him and he bit Marty! King Julien saw Alex was dangerous and banished him to the far side of the island, where the fossa lived.

Meanwhile, after deciding Antarctica wasn't for them, the Penguins arrived on the island of Madagascar. Marty saw this was a chance to help Alex return to New York.

Marty tried to convince his friend to go back to the zoo, but Alex was so worried about attacking him that he refused. The other Zoosters chased after Marty but got trapped by the fossa!

Just as the fossa attacked, Alex appeared and scared them off. The Penguins helped Alex overcome his hunger by making him sushi instead of steak. And the Lemurs threw a big party as the Zoosters prepared to sail back to New York. Little did they know the ship had run out of fuel!

MADAGASCAR MUST-SEES

King Julien's top sight-seeing tips!

👑 Make sure you see me if you can. I'm an amazing king.

👑 If you can't see me, Madagascar has beautiful beaches to look at too. But they're not as beautiful as me.

👑 Steer clear of the fossa. They are annoying, interrupt parties, and rip off limbs.

SNACK ATTACK!

Alex likes sushi and eats it instead of steak. Can you spot the fake fish names below?

1. LIONFISH

2. QUEEN ANGELFISH

3. MONKEY FISH

4. BUTTERFLYFISH

5. CIRCUS FISH

Answer: 3 and 5 are made up.

ALL ABOARD!

Welcome to the Penguin Cruises voyage from Madagascar to New York City.

You'll be sailing on our modern Penguin Liner, which has just returned from a journey to Antarctica. Passengers will be given a colourful garland of flowers as they board, and welcomed by the ship's crew.*
* Unless we're sunbathing!

We have crates of tasty fresh fruit and fish to eat on the voyage. And in case of an emergency, comfortable crate-lifeboats for all passengers.

Thanks for sailing with Penguin Cruises.

We won't give you excuses – we'll give you results!*
* If we can find gas for the boat!

MEET THE CREW

SKIPPER
The ship's Captain, Skipper, is in charge and will oversee your whole cruise.

KOWALSKI
Got a problem? Just ask the ship's host, Kowalski. He'll sort it if he can!

RICO
The boat's chef, Rico, can create tasty meals from almost anything.

PRIVATE
This plucky penguin, Private, helps make guests happy and comfortable.

SKIPPER

KOWALSKI

RICO

PRIVATE

ALEX'S WISH LIST

WISH 1: FOOD
I keep dreaming about steak, and seaweed on a stick just doesn't cut it. The sushi the Penguins make isn't too bad, but some steak would be great ...

WISH 2: PEOPLE
Being in the wild is OK, but I really miss the people who used to look after us at the zoo. There's not even a Supervisor here!

WISH 3: PAVEMENTS
Ever since we arrived I've been stubbing my paws on rocks, stepping on thorns or tripping over logs. This open plan thing really doesn't work for me!

WISH 4: PAMPERING
My mane is getting messy and there's no one here to take care of it for me. What would my fans think if they could see me now?

WISH 5: WATER
The sea water Marty serves in Casa Del Wild isn't just terrible, it's messy too!

WISH 6: A WAY OUT OF HERE!
I don't want to live in a mud hut or wipe myself with a leaf! I'm almost ready to swim back to New York – and I can't even swim!

WISH 7: FANS
I miss the fans I had at the zoo. They cheered when I roared and were always there for me. The Lemurs cheer sometimes but it's just not the same ...

PARK PUZZLER

When did New York Zoo open?

A. 1864 ☐
B. 1964 ☐
C. 1764 ☐

Answer: A

9

THE NEXT ADVENTURE

The Penguins' ship had run out of gas, but that didn't stop the Zoosters from trying to get back to New York. The Penguins repaired King Julien's plane and the animals were on their way. However, as they flew away from Madagascar, the penguin pilots spotted something was up — they were out of fuel! The animals crash-landed in the middle of a savannah and while the Penguins began repairing the plane, the four friends went exploring.

'The good news is we'll be landing immediately. The bad news is we're crash-landing.'

The Zoosters saw some tourists in a truck, but when Alex asked for help, Nana, an old lady, whacked him with her handbag! As the tourists drove off, the Zoosters spotted animals at a nearby water hole and walked over. 'Alakay? Is that you?' gasped a lioness, staring at the birthmark on Alex's paw. Zuba the lion held up his paw to show the same birthmark. They were his parents! Alex had been stolen by poachers in Africa when he was a lion cub, and ended up living in New York.

The Zoosters soon settled into their new home. Melman became the giraffes' witch doctor, Gloria had met some nice hippos and Marty was welcomed into a herd of zebras — who looked and sounded exactly like him! Meanwhile, the Penguins were busy finding parts to repair the plane — by stealing trucks from tourists.

Just as things were looking good, an evil lion, called Makunga, pointed out that if Alex didn't pass the coming of age ceremony, Zuba would have to banish him. Alex thought it was a talent show and jumped at the chance to strut his stuff. But, at the ceremony, Alex soon realised it wasn't a dance-off and ended up plastered to a boulder!

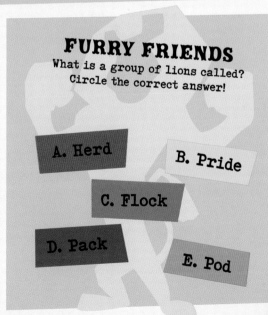

FURRY FRIENDS
What is a group of lions called?
Circle the correct answer!

A. Herd

B. Pride

C. Flock

D. Pack

E. Pod

WILD ABOUT THE WILD

Everything went downhill pretty fast for the Zoosters. Zuba couldn't face banishing his son, so Makunga took over as leader and forced Alex to leave the reserve. Gloria argued with Melman about her date with a hunky hippo, Moto Moto. Marty fell out with Alex over a case of mistaken identity. And Melman was convinced he'd caught a deadly witch doctor's disease!

Then – more disaster! – the animals' water hole dried up. Alex offered to find out what had happened, and asked Marty to join him. The friends made up and set off into the jungle. They soon discovered the problem: stranded tourists had blocked the river with a dam! Nana spotted the friends and Alex was caught in a trap, but Marty escaped.

Meanwhile, King Julien had convinced everyone they could solve the water problem by sacrificing someone in the volcano. Melman, thinking he was dying and had lost Gloria, said he'd do it. But luckily Gloria managed to stop him by explaining how she felt!

Back in the jungle, just as the tourists were about to cook Alex, Zuba burst into the camp and set him free. Nana attacked them but Alex started dancing so the tourists would recognise him. 'It's Alex the lion!' they gasped. Zuba saw that dancing could be useful and started copying Alex's moves — they went down a storm!

Nana wasn't impressed. She grabbed a rifle and fired! A metal barrel swung down and blocked the bullet. It was Marty, Melman and Gloria on the monkey-powered plane! The lions jumped into the barrel and the plane flew off, smashing into the dam and releasing the trapped water!

A giant wave flooded into the water hole, filling it back up. 'My son saved us!' shouted Zuba. 'Three cheers for Alakay!' cried everyone. Alex had completed the Rite Of Passage and Zuba was reinstated as pride leader!

TRUE OR FALSE?
Africa's Victoria Falls is the planet's largest waterfall.

BE A SHOW STOPPER!
Alex's guide to putting on a top dance show . . .

- Get a stage name like mine — The King Of New York!
- Shake it out and loosen up before you go on stage.
- Practise your dance moves, but don't be afraid to freestyle!
- Remember, a good dance performance comes straight from the heart.
- Most importantly, don't get a dance-off confused with a fight when you're taking part in a ceremony. It's really embarrassing!

Answer: True

WISH YOU WERE HERE!

To everyone at New York Zoo,

Hope you're all well and the zoo is good?
We were on our way home to see you in the Penguins'
plane, but it crash-landed in Africa.

It turns out this place is pretty awesome. Marty has been
hanging out with a herd of cool zebras (they all look
really similar), the giraffes here have made Melman
their witch doctor (he's loving it!) and Gloria has met
someone special: Melman! She says it's crazy she's gone
halfway round the world to find out her perfect guy
lived next door! Plus — prepare to be blown away by this
news — I've met my parents! They're called Florrie and
Zuba and it's like I've known them my whole life.

Anyway, better go. There's always so much to do here!
We all miss you and hope to see you soon!

All the best,

Alex The Lion

New York Zoo

New York

NY 10065

USA

The best
zoo in the
world!

WATER WATCH!

Watering hole gone dry? Don't worry, the self-proclaimed King of the Lemurs is here to help ...

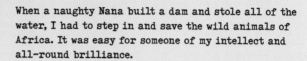

When a naughty Nana built a dam and stole all of the water, I had to step in and save the wild animals of Africa. It was easy for someone of my intellect and all-round brilliance.

Here's my handy guide for if you ever get stuck in the wild with nothing to drink. It's very easy to follow!

1. Make sure all the water really has dried up. Get one of your followers to investigate the watering hole. Have a rest while they do this.

2. If someone suggests the problem is a clogged pipe, let them go and check it out. They will be wrong, but it'll be good to get them out of the way.

3. As I told the animals of Africa, in a situation like this there's only one way to get the precious water back: you must make a small sacrifice to my good friends, the Water Gods, in a nearby volcano.

4. 'But what does that do, my beloved King Julien?' you ask. Well, the sacrifice goes into the volcano, where it's eaten by the friendly Gods. They'll say, 'Thanks very much! That was a tasty sacrifice!' and will give you some water because they're so grateful.

WHAT YOU'LL NEED ...

- A volcano
- A hero to be eaten by Gods
- Someone wonderful (like me) to organise everything

If anyone says throwing a giraffe into a volcano to make water is crazy, explain there's a 50/50 chance it will work. It's pretty solid science. However, if you don't have a hero to sacrifice and someone has built a dam, breaking it will probably do the trick too.

THE ADVENTURE CONTINUES ...EUROPE'S MOST WANTED!

When Alex makes a birthday wish to return to New York, his best friends all want to go too. But they can't get there without the Penguins, so the Zoosters set off to fetch them from Monte Carlo ...

The Penguins have been busy cheating at gambling with help from the Chimps and an elaborate disguise.

But when the Zoosters crash into the casino to get the Penguins, everyone there goes crazy. The police call Animal Control, and their top officer, Captain Dubois, sets out to catch the animals!

The animals race off in the Penguins' Luxury Assault Recreational Vehicle with Captain Dubois in hot pursuit!

It's close, but the Zoosters manage to escape by convincing the animals on a travelling circus to let them hide on their train.

With the police and Animal Control out to capture them, will the friends manage to lay low until the heat dies down? And will they ever see New York again?

FIND OUT WHAT HAPPENS ON PAGE 86!

MARTY'S GREAT BIRTHDAY GUIDE

How to have a crack-a-lackin celebration!

PARTY TIME!
Throw a surprise party like I did for Alex. Just make sure your friend doesn't fall down a hill on the way there like mine did!

GREAT GIFT!
Make your buddy feel brilliant by making them something special. I made a model of New York City from mud for Alex and he loved it!

TOP TREATS!
Bake your friend a cake and put candles on it so they can make a birthday wish. Don't let lemurs hide in it though — it's very messy!

BIG TOP TEASER
Can you work out which two stars don't match the others on this big top tent?

Answers on page 90

OPERATION PENGUIN

PHASE ONE: Break into the casino and grab the Penguins. Get them to take us back to New York in the Monkey-powered super-plane.

PHASE TWO: Tell the Penguins off for abandoning us in Africa.

PHASE THREE: Apologise to the Penguins for overly-hard telling off. Make sure we get our point across though.

PHASE FOUR: Fly back to New York City.

REMIND EVERYONE TO BE:

> INVISIBLE
> STEALTHY
> SILENT

Especially Marty!

REMEMBER! Animals aren't allowed in the casino, so the Chimps will be in disguise!

LOOK OUT FOR ...
The Chimps — the Penguins will be nearby!

EQUIPMENT CHECK LIST

Equipment bag ☐
Spear gun ☐
Fishing pole ☐
Life vest ☐

SHADOW SHAKEDOWN

The lights have gone out in the casino!
Can you spot the real Zoosters from their shadows?

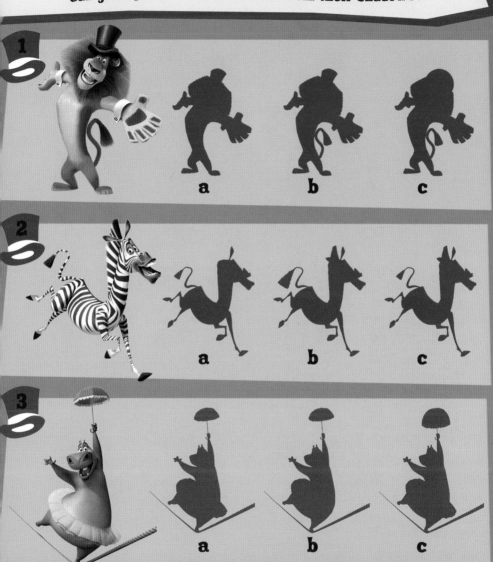

Answers on page 90

ALEX

Description:	Lion
Distinguishing features:	Big glossy mane and a dazzling smile
Home:	Africa and New York Zoo
Likes:	His friends, performing for an audience, roaring, and eating steak or sushi
Dislikes:	Being hungry and letting his pals down
Fast fact:	Alex has a birthmark on his paw, which is the shape of Africa!
Most likely to say:	'A great dance performance comes from the heart!'

TRAPEZE AMERICANO FOR BEGINNERS

🎀 Use your teeth, hands or feet to grab each bar. Do whatever it takes to keep swinging – just don't fall!

🎀 If you do fall, pretend bouncing off the safety net is a special move!

🎀 Don't be afraid of letting your trapeze partner catch you if you fall – it'll look like part of the act!

DID YOU KNOW?

Alex thought King Julien was a squirrel when they first met!

ACTION HERO

Alex has had some really claw-some moments!

Alex scared the fossa off for good when he towered over them and roared, 'This is my territory and I don't ever want to see you on this side of the island again!'
ACTION RATING 4/5

He may have been caught in a trap, but Alex didn't forget about his friends when he was hanging upside down in the jungle. 'Run Marty!' he yelled. 'Go get help!'
ACTION RATING 3/5

Dropping down into the casino doesn't quite go to plan! All Alex wants is to grab the Penguins, but things get a LOT more complicated ...
ACTION RATING 4/5

When Dubois tries to stop the animals escaping on the Chimps' super-plane, Alex races into action. He slices through the noose she puts round Melman's neck and sends her flying!
ACTION RATING 5/5

Coming up with the moves for Trapeze Americano is easier than Alex expects. He panics and uses his teeth, hits his head, and keeps falling into the safety net!
ACTION RATING 4/5

SPOT THE DIFFERENCE

Can you find the 8 differences between these snapshots?

1

2

Answers on page 90

MARTY

Description:	Zebra
Distinguishing features:	Black with white stripes ... or white with black stripes?
Home:	New York Zoo
Likes:	Having fun, hanging out with his friends, other zebras, and running in the wild
Dislikes:	Being told all zebras look similar and being mistaken for another zebra
Fast fact:	Marty built a cabana on Madagascar and served seaweed on a stick there!
Most likely to say:	'Let's go for it!'

DID YOU KNOW?
A zebra's stripes are like fingerprints – no two are exactly the same.

Marty builds Alex's mud model of New York City from memory. 'I made it from crazy obsessive memory!' he grins.

When Stefano is blasted from a cannon, straight towards a cliff face, Marty leaps into action to save him and realises he loves flying. 'Forget about being part of the herd,' he smiles. 'I'm going to be part of the flock!'

The silliest of the Zoosters, Marty is always ready to have fun – even if he's in the middle of a secret mission.

MOTOR WITH MARTY!

Three steps to being a top driver . . .

1. Try to drive in a straight line. Swerving can be dangerous and lead to crashing – especially if you're steering with hooves!

2. Keep your eyes on the road, even if you're arguing with a passenger.

3. Make sure your vehicle has brakes. They come in very handy!

PROFILE

MARTY: NUMBER ONE FRIEND
Find out why he's the best buddy you could ever have!

He's... FUNNY
Which other Zooster would paint themselves with multi-coloured dots and wear a silly afro wig when they're meant to be lying low?
FRIEND SCORE: 5/5

He's... FRIENDLY
Marty may have thought Alex was a show-off when he first arrived at the zoo, but the pair still became best friends. Even if Marty still thinks Alex is a show-off!
FRIEND SCORE: 4/5

He's... ENTHUSIASTIC
When it comes to joining in, Marty is always up for fun. Just don't bother him if he's daydreaming. Like he says, 'If a zebra's in the zone, leave him alone!'
FRIEND SCORE: 5/5

He's... UNDERSTANDING
Even when Alex bit him on the butt, Marty didn't hold it against his friend and gave him the benefit of the doubt.
FRIEND SCORE: 5/5

CONCLUSION
Marty is an amazing zebra, and a brilliant friend. Who wouldn't want to hang out with someone so great?

ODD MARTY OUT

One of these pictures of Marty is different from the rest. Can you work out which one?

GLORIA

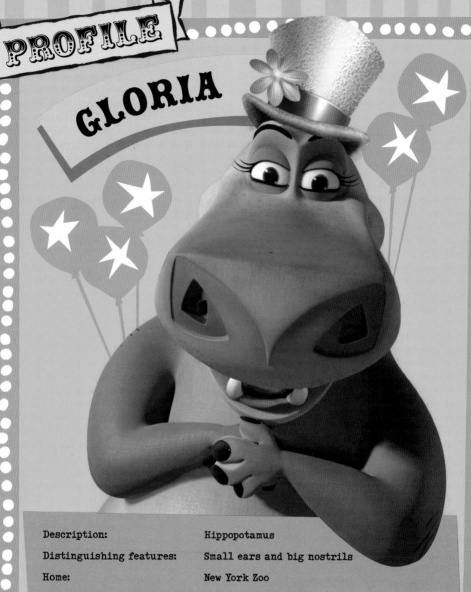

Description:	Hippopotamus
Distinguishing features:	Small ears and big nostrils
Home:	New York Zoo
Likes:	Being with Melman, dancing, and her friends
Dislikes:	Being shushed when she's speaking her mind
Fast fact:	Gloria can sleep anywhere – even on a plane that's crash-landing!
Most likely to say:	'We're New Yorkers: we're tough and gritty!'

Just as the Zoosters move in to grab the Penguins from the casino, she steps onto the glass skylight – with disastrous results!

As the friends are chased by the police and Animal Control, Gloria is the first to realise it was much easier to blend in when they were in Africa.

Now she's realised Melman is the one for her, Gloria will do anything to protect him – even crossing a tiny tightrope to dance with him!

TRUE OR FALSE?

Hippos can't swim. They're so heavy they sink in water.

GLORIA'S GUIDE TO LOOKING GOOD

Want to look as gorgeous as Gloria? Just follow these handy hints . . .

TREAT YOURSELF
Start each day with breakfast in bed! I have six loaves of wheat toast with butter on both sides, and no crusts. You might not need quite as much as me though!

ENJOY BEAUTY
Surrounding myself with beautiful things makes me feel great. I love looking at my favourite flowers, white orchids, and Melman. Yes, that's right, Melman.

TAKE CARE
Want my number one beauty secret? Take a smelly, hot mud bath every day. Wallowing in mud for hours is what makes my skin glow.

BE A BELIEVER
Believe in yourself and always speak your mind. It'll make you look confident and cool – just like me!

GO GLORIA!
Which of these things isn't the heavenly hippo good at?

SINGING

SWIMMING

TIGHTROPE WALKING

SLEEPING

DANCING

Answer: None – Gloria's good at them all!

WILD WORD GAME

Add a letter to the middle column of each line so that it forms a word on either side. Do it correctly and you'll reveal one of Gloria's favourite places!

SWI __ INE

MEN __ GLY

GOL __ EEP

BLO __ LUE

COL __ RMS

FOO __ ALL

BAT __ EAT

PROFILE

MELMAN

Description:	**Giraffe**
Distinguishing features:	**A long neck, friendly smile and a healthy glow – even though Melman always think he looks sickly!**
Home:	**New York Zoo**
Likes:	**Visiting the doctor, especially Dr Goldberg at the zoo, and hanging out with Gloria**
Dislikes:	**Finding brown spots on his body – even though he's covered in them!**
Fast fact:	**Melman says Gloria is the perfect woman and he would do anything for her**
Most likely to say:	**'I'm not feeling well!'**

MELMAN'S PROUDEST MOMENTS

SURVIVING THE WILD

When the friends landed on Madagascar, Melman thought he was doomed and dug himself a grave. After all, he saw twenty-six health code violations as soon as they got there! But he made it through alive and even learnt to like being in the wild.

DOCTOR'S ORDERS

Melman loved being the giraffes' official witch doctor when the Zoosters went to Africa. He was proud to help his new friends and really enjoyed patching everyone up — until he thought he had a deadly witch doctor's disease that is!

SPLASH DOWN

Thinking he was dying and had lost Gloria to Moto Moto, Melman almost sacrificed himself to King Julien's Water Gods. Luckily Gloria stopped him!

TOP TIGHTROPE

He's tried learning to dance, but Melman thinks he can't do it. He's really proud when he manages to dance with Gloria — especially as it's on a tightrope!

Having a long neck means Melman is the perfect lookout when the gang are being chased by Captain Dubois!

DID YOU KNOW?

At nearly six metres, the giraffe is the world's tallest animal.

Melman discovers he can tightrope walk – and dance – by accident! And it's all thanks to Gloria's help.

FEAR FACTOR

Which of these tongue-twisting phobias does Melman have?

WEIRD WORD	FRIGHTENED OF
1. Blennophobia	Slime
2. Lutraphobia	Otters
3. Metrophobia	Poetry
4. Geliophobia	Laughter
5. Lachanophobia	Vegetables
6. Genuphobia	Knees
7. Anthophobia	Flowers
8. Peladophobia	Baldness
9. Acrophobia	Heights
10. Phobophobia	Phobias

Answer: 9

NAME GAME

See if you can fit the names of the
Madagascar buddies into the spaces below.

GLORIA

ALEX

JULIEN

A
L
E
X

MORT

MAURICE

MARTY

MELMAN

Answers on page 90

KING JULIEN

Description:	Lemur
Distinguishing features:	Prominent crown, big eyes and a royal swagger
Home:	Madagascar
Likes:	Bossing Maurice about, conquering new lands and Sonya the bear
Dislikes:	Not getting own way
Fast fact:	He thought the Zoosters were savage aliens from the future when he first met them!
Most likely to say:	'Please feel free to bask in my glow!'

JULIEN'S WORDS OF WISDOM

The funny lemur always has something to say for himself . . .

'I have an empire to expand. I have assistants who depend on me to kick them.'

'Maurice! Announce my arrival to the people from Clandestine! The Clandestines await me!'

'Shhh, we're hiding. Everyone needs to be quiet . . . Shhh! Who's making that noise? Oh, it's me again . . .'

'I'm flying, I'm flying! I'm the first flying monkey!'

'Come on, time to robot! I am robot king of the monkey thing . . . compute . . . compute!'

'Ha, ha, ha! I like laughing! It's such a nice experience!'

King Julien is always up for going to new places. It's only fair that as many people as possible should meet someone so amazing!

They might not always see eye to eye, but King Julien likes Sonya so much, he can't imagine life without her — even if she does squash him sometimes!

When King Julien thinks the paparazzi are after a picture in Monte Carlo, he throws open the doors of the LARV and does some serious posing. He's definitely not camera-shy!

CROWNING GLORY!

Top tips to look great in a crown from His Royal Lemur-ness . . .

👑 Be fantastic! Like me, King Julien!

👑 Wear your crown on your head. They don't look good anywhere else.

👑 Put a gecko on your crown and get him dancing!

MAURICE

Description:	Lemur
Distinguishing features:	Big ears and a white patch of fur on his chest
Home:	Madagascar
Likes:	Helping King Julien, and giving good advice
Dislikes:	Being bossed about by King Julien and having his advice ignored
Fast fact:	It took Maurice a while to get used to the Zoosters — especially Alex
Most likely to say:	'Presenting your royal highness, our illustrious King Julian the XIII . . . self-proclaimed lord of the lemurs, etc, etc, hooray, everybody!'

MAURICE'S ROYAL DUTIES

- Tell King Julien whatever he wants to hear
- Fix whatever King Julien breaks
- Advise King Julien on his cunning plans
- Comb the knots from King Julien's tail

MORT

Description:	Mouse lemur
Distinguishing features:	Big eyes, cute little ears and a big bushy tail
Home:	Madagascar
Likes:	King Julien and King Julien's feet
Dislikes:	Being used as bait for the fossa on Madagascar
Fast fact:	Mort loves being one of the gang — he even jumps out of Alex's birthday cake
Most likely to say:	'Yay!' He's always very enthusiastic!

PROFILE

SKIPPER

Description:	Penguin
Home:	New York Zoo
Likes:	Sushi, karate and being the leader of the Penguins
Dislikes:	Antarctica – all of the Penguins thought it was too bleak and windy
Fast fact:	Skipper buys gold teeth so he can eat apples, but then doesn't like the taste of them!
Most likely to say:	'Progress report!' This plucky little guy likes to stay on top of the Penguins' adventures

PRIVATE

Description:	Penguin
Home:	New York Zoo
Likes:	Cracking codes and pillow fights
Dislikes:	Letting his team down
Fast fact:	Private has a British accent, which Skipper says is fake!
Most likely to say:	'Yes, sir!' Private is so eager, he'll do anything for Skipper's team

RICO

Description: Penguin
Home: New York Zoo
Likes: Making sushi and blowing things up
Dislikes: Missions going wrong
Fast fact: The Penguins' weapons expert has a feathery mohawk and a scar on his beak!
Most likely to say: Very little – Rico is a bird of few words!

KOWALSKI

Description: Penguin
Home: New York Zoo
Likes: Being Skipper's second-in-command
Dislikes: Rushing plans for a mission
Fast fact: Kowalski is a brainbox when it comes to science
Most likely to say: Something smart – he's a genius!

MADAGASCAR MIX-UP

Can you spot the odd ones out in the rows below?

1

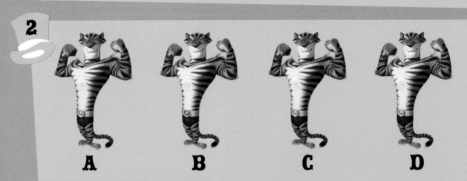

A   B   C   D

2

3

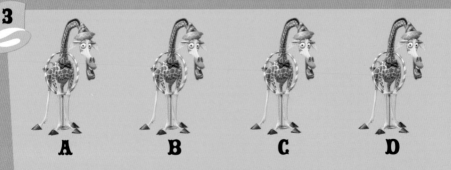

A   B   C   D

Answers on page 90

TRUE OR FALSE?

See how well you know the Madagascar
gang with our tricky quiz . . .

		TRUE	FALSE
1	Alex's parents called him Alakay.	☐	☐
2	King Julien gave his first crown to Maurice.	☐	☐
3	Melman taught Gloria to dance.	☐	☐
4	The animals first left their zoo because of Marty.	☐	☐
5	The Penguins built a hot air balloon to travel to Africa.	☐	☐

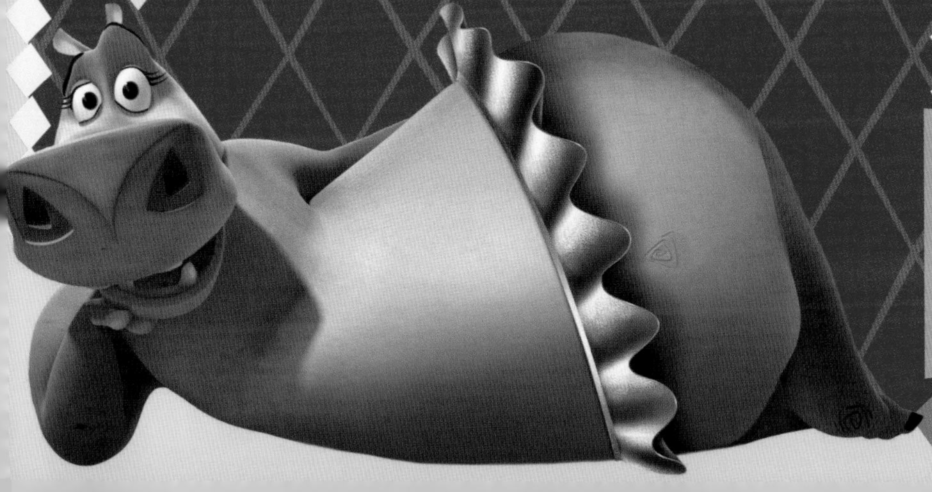

Answers on page 90

43

MASON

Description: Chimpanzee
Home: New York Zoo
Likes: Poetry, fancy food and art
Dislikes: Messiness – Mason likes being neat and tidy
Fast fact: He understands sign-language and explains what Phil says
Most likely to say: 'Phil! I ought to wash your hands out with soap!' when Phil signs something cheeky!

PHIL

Description: Chimpanzee
Home: New York Zoo
Likes: Lounging about and throwing poo at people
Dislikes: Losing at chess!
Fast fact: Phil likes dressing up and even wore a top hat in Africa!
Most likely to say: Phil can't speak, but he loves reading!

SHOPPING LIST

BANANAS
CHESS SET
WELDING KIT
EXTRA BANANAS
DYNAMITE

MASON AND PHIL'S DISGUISE GUIDE

Find out how the higher mammals with the thumbs go undercover!

HAT'LL DO!
A hat like this with a feather helps make him look even taller!

WIG OUT!
A big wig like this not only makes Phil look human, it makes him seem taller too.

EYE EYE!
Sunglasses cover up Phil's eyes, which might give the game away and reveal his chimp-iness. They look cool too!

MAKE IT UP!
A false nose and lots of thick make-up transforms Phil into the King of Versailles!

GET SWIRLY

The Chimps have changed these pictures to hide who's in them. Can you work out who's who?

A

B

CAPTAIN DUBOIS

Description:	Human
Distinguishing features:	Red lips and a spotless Animal Control uniform
Home:	Monte Carlo, France
Likes:	Hunting, bossing people about, and collecting stuffed beasts
Dislikes:	Animals on the loose
Fast fact:	She's so desperate to catch the Zoosters, Captain Dubois wrestles a deadly black mamba snake to get its poisonous venom!
Most likely to say:	'Get out of my way, you fool! I'm tracking animals!'

 PROFILE

ANIMAL CONTROL
OFFICER APPLICATION

OFFICIAL

Name: Captain Chantel Dubois

ID photo:

How much do you like animals?

I don't like animals ☐
A little ☐
Very much ☑ *Stuffed on my wall!*

How do you feel when you see a wild animal?

Happy ☐
Alert ☑
Disgusted ☑

Please finish these sentences

Animals belong ... *on my wall!*
Being an Animal Control Officer ... *is what I was born to do!*
I should get this job because ... *it would give me great job satisfaction!*

Please score your abilities (1 to 10)

Fitness   10
Tracking skills 10+
Sense of smell   20!
Eyesight   10+
Driving   10 *especially on a scooter!*

ADDITIONAL NOTES

I have always wanted to be an Animal Control Officer, and am determined to become the BEST there has ever been! My dream is to have big game to catch as this will really test me.

Signature
Captain Dubois

APPROVED

Animal Control Officer Kit

✳ Tranquillizer dart gun
✳ Animal Control Officer badge
✳ Leather gloves
✳ Telescope snare
✳ Gold lapel studs
✳ Spare keys for scooter

Captain Dubois will stop at nothing to catch the Zoosters. The Animal Control Officer even breaks out of jail after she's arrested for tranquillizing three police officers.

Tracking animals is one of Captain Dubois' top talents. She has an amazing sense of smell and can sniff out almost anything — including Alex and his friends!

Things look bad for the animals when Captain Dubois shows up at the New York Zoo. But will the Zoosters manage to escape once and for all?

WHERE'S THE WORD?

Can you choose the right word to complete these Captain Dubois quotes?

1 'When I was seven I strangled my first _ _ _ _ _ _'

2 'To catch big game, you bring your big _ _ _ _ '

3 'Poor animals, you should never have left the _ _ _ _ _ _

A. Forest   D. Game
B. Parrot   E. Toilet
C. Socks   F. Gorilla

BEHIND BARS

Can you spot who Captain Dubois has locked up?

A

B

C

D

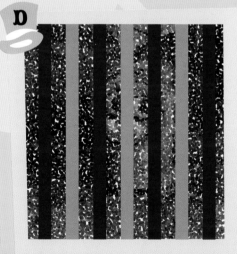

VITALY

Description:	Tiger
Distinguishing features:	Stripy coat and lots of muscles!
Home:	Circus Zaragoza
Likes:	Making borscht and old traditions
Dislikes:	Performing – the macho Russian tiger lost his passion for the circus when his act went wrong
Fast fact:	Vitaly didn't trust Alex when they first met because his mane was too big and glossy!
Most likely to say:	'Nyet!' Vitaly usually says 'no' to everything!

Vitaly doesn't want to help the Zoosters and says they aren't welcome on the train because they're not circus animals.

Could Vitaly discover his passion for performing with Alex's help? Or will he get burnt again?

Circus Zaragoza's biggest star, Vitaly used to wow the world by squeezing through impossibly small hoops. But then his act went up in smoke — literally!

TOP TRICK

Which of these wouldn't help Vitaly squeeze through his hoops?

A Banana milkshake
B Hair conditioner
C Olive oil

ROLL UP! ROLL UP!

Get ready for the ~~best~~ show in the world with . . .

WORST!

CIRCUS ZARAGOZA!

Introducing . . .

You'll gasp as he drops all of his juggling balls!

What's amazing about rolling over and standing up?

PLUS! VITALY, the World's Strongest Tiger!

This guy was on fire — literally!

STEFANO! The juggling sea lion!

GIA! The amazing jaguar!

PLUS! Exciting elephants!
Sensational steeds!
And much more!

If you're unlucky!

COMING TO A TOWN NEAR YOU!

CIRCUS SUDOKU

Complete the puzzle so that each row of six squares, each column of six squares, and each coloured section of six squares contains all the letters in the word VITALY.

L		Y			V
	T				
I			T		L
			Y		
	L				
V		T		I	

GIA

Description:	Jaguar
Distinguishing features:	Sleek coat and big brown eyes
Home:	Circus Zaragoza
Likes:	Performing and learning Trapeze Americano
Dislikes:	Being be spied on, and quitters
Fast fact:	The circus means everything to Gia, and she'll do anything to make it a success
Most likely to say:	'Circus stick together!'

CIRCUS STARDOM

Want to perform with the Zoosters? You'll need at least three of these cool qualities . . .

**CONFIDENCE
ENERGY
SILLINESS
BRAVERY
CREATIVITY
FOCUS**

The brave jaguar stands up to Vitaly when he doesn't want to help the Zoosters. If it wasn't for her, the Zoosters would have been caught by the police!

Gia catches Alex watching her practise, and the proud jaguar puts him in his place, warning him not to do anything that threatens the circus.

Alex might make it up, but Gia can tell Trapeze Americano could be a big hit — even though Marty crashes into them when they're practising!

SHOWTIME SCRAMBLE

Alex is due on stage with Gia. Can you help him
get back to the circus in time for their act?
Just follow the word GIA as it appears below!

START

G	I	E	A	G	I
I	G	A	P	A	G	I	S	A
A	S	I	S	J	P	M	F	G
G	V	G	H	A	I	G	A	I
I	D	A	I	G	U	F	K	L
A	L	D	M	F	G	I	A	Z
G	I	A	G	I	A	F	G	I
L	R	F	R	N	I	G	Y	A
I	G	A	I	G	A	A	I	G
A	R	U	F	R	H	B	J	L
G	T	O	A	G	I	Y	R	N
I	A	G	I	F	A			YOU MADE IT!

TIGHTROPE TUMBLE

Think you can tackle the tightrope like Melman?
Grab a friend and let your fingers do the talking!

WHAT TO DO

1. Choose who's going first. If it's you, you're the first tightrope walker and must close your eyes and touch the colour dial.

2. The colour chosen is where you must place a finger on the tightrope. Be careful though — you can't move it once it's on there!

3. Now take it in turns to repeat steps one and two, using the same hand to walk the tightrope, until you're both balancing five fingers on it.

4. The winner is the player who can balance on the tightrope for the longest!

STEFANO

Description:	Sea lion
Distinguishing features:	Curly white whiskers
Home:	Circus Zaragoza
Likes:	Having fun, making new friends, and being an entertainer
Dislikes:	Gloomy people
Fast fact:	The Italian sea lion's accent means he pronounces Alex's name 'Alice'!
Most likely to say:	'The show must go on!'

The Zoosters are amazed at how bad the circus is when they see everyone perform. But Stefano is so enthusiastic, he doesn't realise they're disappointed!

Stefano shows Alex the Circus Master's car, and explains Circus Zaragoza was once the most popular circus in Europe.

No challenge is too great for Stefano if it's going to help save the circus. 'I've dreamt of being fired from a cannon since I was a little pup,' he says as Rico adds loads of dynamite.

SPEAK OUT!

The Zoosters do a lot of travelling. See how to say, 'hello' in different languages for when you do too!

WHO	LANGUAGE	SAY . . .
ZUBA	African	Jambo (jam-bo)
STEFANO	Italian	Ciao (ch-ow)
DUBOIS	French	Bonjour (bon-jore)
VITALY	Russian	Привет (pri-vet)

WHAT'S YOUR CIRCUS SKILL?

Tick five statements you agree with, then see which colour you chose the most and find out what your act in the big top would be!

I have nicknames for most of my mates! ☐

Friends say I'm fun to have around ☐

I don't let things get to me ☐

Playing games gets me giggling! ☐

I love theme parks! ☐

I'm always there for my pals ☐

I'm good at planning parties ☐

Most days I'm full of energy ☐

Surprises are sure to get me smiling! ☐

BIG TOP CONCLUSIONS:

Mostly BLUE ...
Your circus skill is the tightrope! Your balanced way of looking at the world means you'd be great at walking the tightrope, like Gloria and Melman!

Mostly RED ...
Your circus skill is being fired from a cannon! You love thrills and spills, and would be great at performing an amazing cannon act, like Stefano and Marty!

Mostly YELLOW ...
Your circus skill is the trapeze! Your laid-back, kind personality makes you the perfect type of person to be a trapeze star, like Alex and Gia!

Description: Black bear
Distinguishing features: Small ears, huge body and a big tuft of fur on the top of her head
Home: Circus Zaragoza
Likes: Riding her tricycle, eating fish and wearing tutus
Dislikes: Breaking her tricycle and not getting her own way
Fast fact: The travelling circus's most ferocious animal, Sonya casts a spell on King Julien, who is instantly smitten with her
Most likely to say: 'Brwaaal!' She is a bear after all!

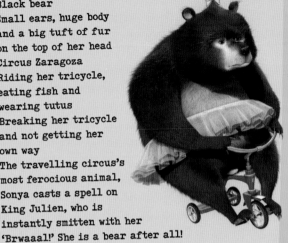

CIRCUS DOGS

Description: Terriers
Distinguishing features: Wet noses and wagging tails
Home: Circus Zaragoza
Likes: Excitement, thrills and their rocket skates!
Dislikes: Being called cute
Fast fact: They may look sweet and innocent but these hounds, and the other Dancing Dogs, are wild hooligans!
Most likely to say: 'Naff off you muppet!'

DID YOU KNOW?
Circus Maximus in Ancient Rome could seat 250,000 people!

PROFILE

THE AMAZING ANDALUSIANS

Description:	White horses
Distinguishing features:	Beautiful long manes and big blue eyes
Home:	Circus Zaragoza
Likes:	Prancing, looking glamorous and giving makeovers
Dislikes:	Getting distracted and eating hay in the middle of a performance
Fast fact:	Esmarelda, Esperanza and Ernstina are beautiful horse triplets from Spain who look, sound and dress exactly alike
Most likely to say:	'We're going to paint you pink!'

PERFECT PROPS

Which equipment wouldn't be used at a circus?

1. UNICYCLE
2. DUSTBIN
3. STILTS
4. TRAPEZE
5. PARACHUTE
6. JUGGLING BALLS

CIRCUS SPOTTER!

Cross out all of the letters that appear more than once and,
reading from left to right, the remaining letters will reveal
one of the most popular acts in Circus Zaragoza . . .

B	T	C	R	X
A	S	Q	M	W
F	P	D	H	K
D	H	O	K	L
X	I	F	Q	C
W	B	N	S	E

A-Z OF MADAGASCAR

Check out our 26 facts about the Zoosters and their friends . . .

A is for ALEX

Whether he's in New York or the circus, this furry fella is a star!

B is for BIG TOP

Whatever country they're in, this is where the Circus Zaragoza performances take place!

C is for CIRCUS

A travelling circus is the perfect cover for the Zoosters to get back to New York.

D is for DUBOIS

Animal Control Officer Captain Dubois is pretty scary and means business.

E is for ESMARELDA

This circus horse and her friends, Ernstina and Esperanza give Marty a crazy makeover!

F is for FUR POWER

Marty chanted this to get the circus animals excited about revamping their show!

G is for GIA

This talented jaguar loves learning about Trapeze Americano from Alex.

H is for HIPPO

Beautiful and smart, Gloria the hippo can't wait to tightrope walk with Melman!

I is for ITALY

The Zoosters realise the circus is in trouble during the show in Rome.

J is for JULIEN

King Julien doesn't know what to do when Sonya refuses to leave the circus.

K is for KOWALSKI

This penguin will do anything for his friends, Rico, Skipper and Private.

L is for LEMURS

Maurice and Mort are far from Madagascar, but will always help their King.

M is for MELMAN

The sickly, accident-prone giraffe is worried Gloria will find out he can't dance!

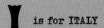

N is for NEW YORK

Alex is homesick, so the Zoosters decide to visit the Big Apple for a holiday!

O is for OCEAN

The new friends sail across the Atlantic Ocean for an important show in America.

P is for PENGUINS

From thrilling rescue missions to sneaky spying, the Penguins are always ready for action!

Q is for QUEEN

King Julien wants his new love, Sonya the bear, to be his queen!

R is for RICH

The Penguins team-up with the Chimps to make lots of money in France. Ker-ching!

S is for STEFANO

This friendly sea lion encourages Vitaly to help the Zoosters.

T is for TRAIN

Alex and his friends see the Circus Zaragoza train carriage just as the police are about to catch them!

U is for UNDERCOVER

The Chimps play roulette disguised as the King of Versailles!

V is for VITALY

This circus tiger lost his fame and fur in an accident on stage. But can he make a comeback?

W is for WISH

The adventure begins when Alex makes a birthday wish to visit New York Zoo.

X is for EXCITING

The animals must make their circus as exciting as possible to impress a promoter!

Y is for YACHTS

The Zoosters are surrounded by yachts in Monte Carlo as they look for the Penguins.

Z is for ZEBRA

Marty is a fun-loving dreamer. He even teams up with Stefano for an amazing cannon act!

KING JULIEN'S GUIDE TO ROMANCE

When King Julien met Sonya, it was love at first sight.
Here are the romantic lemur's top tips for falling in love . . .

BE CHARMING

When I first met Sonya I wowed her with my royal charm. She was bowled over when I told her she looked like a fat, hairy super model who smells. How could she resist me?

PAY COMPLIMENTS

In the middle of telling me how beautiful I am, Maurice mentioned people like hearing compliments. So I always tell Sonya what I like about her. For instance, I often remind her she has a very hairy back, which is something I like in a woman.

SPOIL THE ONE YOU LOVE

People say you can't buy love, but they are WRONG! Sonya loved the ring and motorbike I gave her in Italy. They made her love me more or my name isn't King Julien XIII. That is my name isn't it?

GET LOVEY DOVEY

Being such a brilliant King means people love me as soon as they meet me, but I made sure Sonya fell for me by telling her I wanted to kiss every inch of her huge head. Even though it could take me a number of weeks.

REMEMBER TO BUY . . .

- ♥ New red ball for Sonya to roll about on
- ♥ Stool to stand on when I'm talking to Sonya
- ♥ New tricycle for Sonya
- ♥ Bucket of fish heads – Sonya loves these tasty snacks!

SPOTLIGHT SEARCH

Can you see who's about to be the centre
of attention in the big top?

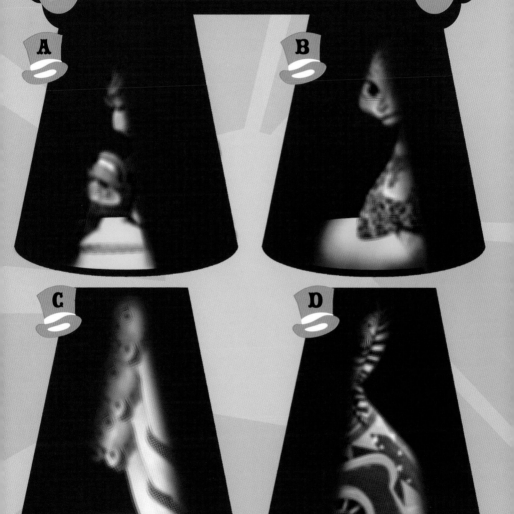

A

B

C

D

Answers on page 90

CIRCUS SMASH

Can you work out which of the missing pieces will complete the picture?

WHO SAID THAT?

Can you match the Zoosters to what they said?

1 'It took an African volcano to bring us together!'

2 'That is one ugly, magugly lady!'

3 'Don't just sit there, fancy-pants! Grab the wheel!'

4 'You'd rather swallow a broom than dance, Melman?'

5 'Trapeze Americano is extremely difficult. It's not teachable!'

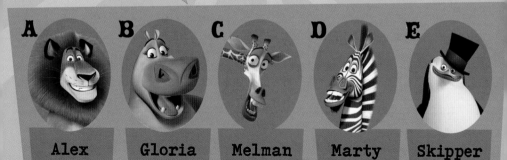

A Alex

B Gloria

C Melman

D Marty

E Skipper

Answers on page 90

CIRCUS ZARAGOZA HANDBOOK

Want to be a hit in the big top? These handy hints from the circus stars will help . . .

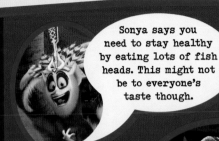

Sonya says you need to stay healthy by eating lots of fish heads. This might not be to everyone's taste though.

Use new equipment. W love our rock powered skat

Believe in yourself! I couldn't dance or tightrope walk, but I soon did both without realising it!

Be brave! My act would be nothing if I didn't try to achieve the impossible Steer clear of using extra virgin olive oil in your act though – it's far too flammable!

Dare to be different! People want amazing new acts – like Trapeze Americano! Where else can you see a lion with a jet pack jumping into a pool of acid and cobras?

CIRCUS DO'S AND DON'TS

DO
★ Put on the best show possible
★ Complete your dance routine
★ Keep your cool onstage

DON'T
★ Stop to eat hay in the middle of your act
★ Start chasing your tail
★ Sit on little girls in the audience

CRAZY CHASE GAME!

Think you can escape Captain Dubois and her Animal Control Officers? Play this game to find out!

HOW TO PLAY

◆ The game is for two to four players.

◆ Use the four counters on page 95 or, if you don't want to cut up your book, use coins. You'll need a dice too.

◆ Choose which character you're going to be. Then roll the dice to see who goes first.

◆ The object of the game is to be the first Zooster to reach the Monkey-powered super-plane and escape Captain Dubois.

◆ Be careful though! While some boxes will take you closer to the plane, some of them could land you in last place!

◆ Players must throw the correct number to board the plane, and then throw a six to win the game.

START

King Julien throws open the LARV's back doors to pose for paparazzi. Miss a turn!

5

6

Whoops! Private slips off the gas. Stay put until you throw an even number.

The LARV crashes through road barriers. Move back one space as you try to slow down.

11

12

13

The LARV teeters on the edge of the Hotel Ambassador roof. Miss a go as you try to balance there.

1 Move forward two spaces as you race off in the Penguins' Luxury Assault Recreational Vehicle!

2 Watch out! Dubois is firing at you! Race forward two spaces as you escape her!

4

3 You crash into a sports car. Miss a go as you drive over it!

7 You unleash the Omega-3 slick. Move forward a space as Dubois leaps off her scooter!

8

9

10 Race forward two spaces as you fire up Kowalski's nuclear reactor!

You drive the wrong way down a one-way street. Move back a space as you swerve to avoid cars!

YAY! The LARV has landed on the super-plane! Throw a six to jump on board and win the game!

FINISH

STAGE STAR

Can you help Vitaly construct the smallest hoop for his act using these pieces?

1

2

3

4

5

6

7

8

9

10

11

12

Answers on page 90

CIRCUS MAKEOVER

Want to know how Alex plans to make over Circus Zaragoza? Check out his pin board!

TO DO LIST ...

✸ Get rid of the people! Animals only – fur-power!

✸ Try to convince Melman not to juggle bowling pins. He'll hurt himself!

✸ Help everyone find their own passion for performing!

Watch out for these back stage!

These guys may look the same but they're different on the inside!

They're cute and teensy-weensy, but must see themselves as massive balls of fire!

Give them rocket shoes?

Fire him out of a cannon?

THINGS TO WATCH OUT FOR

1 Animals who are just going through the motions – they need to give more!

2 Any performer who's stuck in a rut.

3 Melman throwing those bowling pins about. They hurt!

The elephants need to believe they're as light as feathers!

PICTURE PERFECT

Only three of these pictures appear in all four
frames. Can you figure out which ones they are?

WHAT'S YOUR MADAGASCAR DESTINATION?

Take this test to see where you'd be happiest hanging out with the Zoosters!

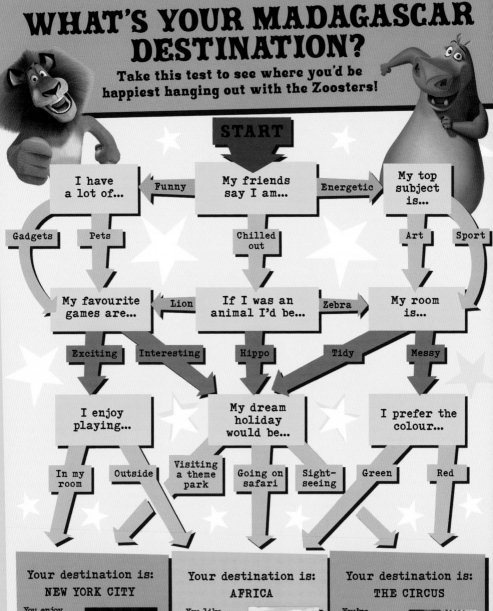

START

I have a lot of... ← Funny — My friends say I am... — Energetic → My top subject is...

Gadgets — Pets — Chilled out — Art — Sport

My favourite games are... ← Lion — If I was an animal I'd be... — Zebra → My room is...

Exciting — Interesting — Hippo — Tidy — Messy

I enjoy playing... — My dream holiday would be... — I prefer the colour...

In my room — Outside — Visiting a theme park — Going on safari — Sight-seeing — Green — Red

---

Your destination is:
NEW YORK CITY

You enjoy being busy, so the hustle and bustle of New York City is for you! Cool!

Your destination is:
AFRICA

You like being near nature and love animals, so Africa is the place for you! Wild!

Your destination is:
THE CIRCUS

You're always full of beans and up for fun, which means you'd love travelling with the circus!

New York Zoo proudly presents . . .

BACK FROM THE WILD!

MARTY THE ZEBRA!

GLORIA THE HIPPO!

MELMAN THE GIRAFFE!

The four animals that mysteriously disappeared on their way to a wildlife preserve in Kenya are BACK! Rescued by Zoo Officials, the animals have been returned to their enclosures, and New York Zoo is throwing hourly parades to celebrate!

And the King of New York City . . .
ALEX THE LION!

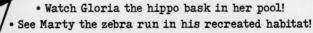

- Watch Gloria the hippo bask in her pool!
- See Marty the zebra run in his recreated habitat!
- Feed Melman the giraffe!*
- Hear Alex the lion roar!

* Unless he has a
doctor's appointment

BACK BY POPULAR DEMAND,
THE KING OF NEW YORK
CITY, ALEX THE LION!

Don't miss!
FREE balloons
and welcome
home parade!

ARE YOU A MADAGASCAR MASTER?

See how much you know about the Zoosters' latest adventure with this tricky quiz!

1 Who has their birthday at the start of Madagascar 3?

a) Alex
b) Marty
c) Melman

2 What country is Vitaly from?

a) Italy
b) France
c) Russia

3 What is Captain Dubois' job?

a) Policewoman
b) Animal Control Officer
c) Scientist

4 Where do the Zoosters first meet the circus animals?

a) Bus
b) Train
c) Car

5 Which country do the Zoosters follow the Penguins to?

a) Germany
b) Spain
c) France

6 Who dressed in disguise to buy the circus?

a) Stefano
b) Sonya
c) The Chimps

7

Which of these isn't
a circus dog?

a) Jonesy
b) Esmarelda
c) Frankie

8

Who keeps calling
Alex, 'Alice'?

a) Stefano
b) Marty
c) Maurice

9

Who tries out the
rocket-powered skates?

a) Alex
b) Gia
c) Jonesy

10

Who tightrope walks
with Melman?

a) Mort
b) Gloria
c) Alex

11

Who is the circus'
trapeze star?

a) Gia
b) Vitaly
c) Maya

12

Where do the animals meet
the circus promoter?

a) Africa
b) London
c) France

NOW SEE HOW YOU SCORED!

Give yourself a point for each correct answer . . .
1A, 2C, 3B, 4B, 5C, 6C, 7B, 8A, 9C, 10B, 11A, 12B

1–4 POINTS
Hey, you know loads
about Madagascar.
Keep watching to
enjoy it even more!

5–8 POINTS
Wow! There's not
much you don't know
about the Zoosters'
adventures, is there?

9–12 POINTS
Amazing! You know
so much about
Madagascar, you got
top marks. Well done!

MOST WANTED WORDSEARCH

Can you find the Madagascar words hidden in this grid?

M	K	M	A	U	R	I	C	E	E	E
E	A	O	A	R	Y	L	A	T	I	V
L	A	D	W	R	I	R	T	A	M	O
M	L	I	A	A	T	C	R	V	A	E
A	E	S	G	G	L	Y	O	I	S	S
N	X	E	W	A	A	S	M	R	O	T
D	U	B	O	I	S	S	K	P	N	E
R	E	P	P	I	K	S	C	I	M	F
C	I	R	C	U	S	F	M	A	F	A
A	I	R	O	L	G	O	N	E	R	N
J	U	L	I	E	N	P	H	I	L	O

ALEX
CIRCUS
DUBOIS
GIA
GLORIA
JULIEN
KOWALSKI
MADAGASCAR

MARTY
MASON
MAURICE
MELMAN

MORT
PHIL

PRIVATE
RICO
SKIPPER
STEFANO
VITALY

Answers on page 90

GUESS WHO

Fancy a laugh? Then try this Madagascar guessing game. You'll just need a friend and a clock to play!

HOW TO PLAY

1. While your opponent looks away, close your eyes and touch this page to choose a character.

2. Now you have 30 seconds to do a funny impression of your chosen character.

3. If your opponent guesses correctly, you get a point and have another go. If your opponent can't tell who you're pretending to be, you get no points and it's their turn. Players get an extra point if their impression makes their opponent laugh!

4. The winner is the player with the most points after 5 minutes!

CONCLUSION

The Zoosters buy
Circus Zaragoza
with the money
from the casino,
and become
friends with the
performers.

After a bad
performance
in Rome, it's
clear the
circus is in
trouble. Alex
asks everyone
to work
together and
they set out
to reinvent
the show.

The animals work hard and it pays off — the new show impresses an important American promoter who signs the circus up to a big deal!

The circus visits New York, where the Zoosters are captured and returned to the zoo! Their new friends help them escape, and Captain Dubois ends up in a crate, sailing to Madagascar!

COLOURING IN

Use your pens to bring these pictures to life!

ANSWERS

Page 17, BIG TOP TEASER

Page 19, SHADOW SHAKEDOWN
1B, 2C, 3A

Page 23, SPOT THE DIFFERENCE

Page 27, ODD MARTY OUT
D

Page 31, WILD WORD GAME

SWI	M	INE
MEN	U	GLY
GOL	D	EEP
BLO	B	LUE
COL	A	RMS
FOO	T	ALL
BAT	H	EAT

Page 35, NAME GAME

```
                        G
                        L
              M    M A U R I C E
    A    M    A    O
J U L I E N  R    R
    E    L    T    I
    X    M O R T Y A
         A    Y
         N
```

Page 42, MADAGASCAR MIX-UP
1. D
2. B
3. A

Page 43, TRUE OR FALSE?
1 True
2 False
3 False
4 True
5 False

Page 45, GET SWIRLY
A King Julien
B Alex

Page 48, WHERE'S THE WORD?
1B, 2D, 3A

Page 49, BEHIND BARS
A. Gloria
B. Melman
C. Alex
D. Mort

Page 51, TOP TRICK
A

Page 53, CIRCUS SUDOKU

L	I	Y	A	T	V
A	T	V	Y	L	I
I	Y	A	T	V	L
T	V	L	I	Y	A
Y	L	I	V	A	T
V	A	T	L	I	Y

Page 56, SHOWTIME SCRAMBLE

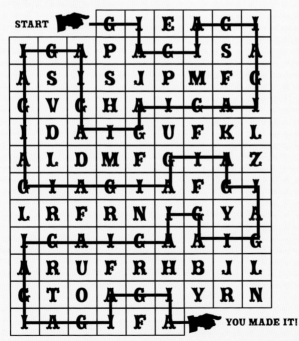

START

YOU MADE IT!

ANSWERS

Page 63, CIRCUS SPOTTER!
Trampoline

Page 69, SPOTLIGHT SEARCH
A. The Chimps
B. Gia
C. The Horses
D. Marty

Page 70, CIRCUS SMASH
A7, B5, C2

Page 72, WHO SAID THAT?
1C
2D
3E
4B
5A

Page 76, STAGE STAR
Sections 2, 4, 8 and 11

Page 78, PICTURE PERFECT

Page 84, MOST WANTED WORDSEARCH

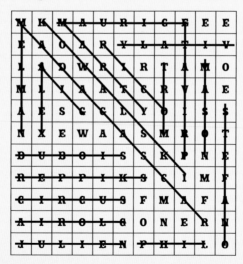

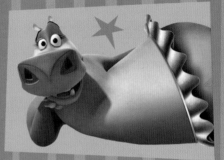

STAMP

STAMP

Counters for page 74